OLD ELM SPEAKS

SPEAKS

TREE POEMS

by Kristine O'Connell George
Illustrated by Kate Kiesler

CLARION BOOKS
New York

Clarion Books
a Houghton Mifflin Company imprint
215 Park Avenue South, New York, NY 10003
Text copyright © 1998 by Kristine O'Connell George
Illustrations copyright © 1998 by Kate Kiesler

The illustrations for this book were executed in oil paint.
The text is set in 16/20-point Goudy.

Printed in Singapore.

Library of Congress Cataloging-in-Publication Data
George, Kristine O'Connell.
    Old Elm speaks : tree poems / by Kristine O'Connell George ;
illustrated by Kate Kiesler.
            p. cm.
    Summary: A collection of short, simple poems which present images
relating to trees in various circumstances and throughout the seasons.
    ISBN 0-395-87611-7
    1. Trees—Juvenile poetry. 2. Children's poetry, American.
[1. Trees—Poetry. 2. American poetry.] I. Kiesler, Kate, ill. II. Title.
PS3557.E48804 1998
811'.54—dc21   97-49333
CIP
AC

TWP 10 9 8 7 6 5 4 3 2 1

For the saplings—
Andy, Brian, Bryanna, Cassie, Christal, Courtney,
Erin, Jake, Joe, Josh, Lauren, Natalie, and Patty—
and in memory of Kari Hildebrand.
—K.O.G.

For Jacques.
—K.K.

Oak's Introduction

I've been wondering
when you'd notice
me standing here.

I've been waiting,
watching you
grow taller.

I have grown too.
My branches
are strong.

Step closer.
Let's see
how high

you can

climb.

Bud

A tiny velveteen satchel,
the color of pale cream,
is perched on the tip
of this bare branch.

Snap open the clasp—
and you will find,
inside this tiny valise,
one rolled and folded
neatly packed

leaf.

Hide and Go Seek

Little sister
thinks that
tree will
hide her.
It is slender;
she is wider.
I pretend
not to see
a very
odd tree
with an

       e
    l
b o w

and a
       k
         n
       e e

8

Celebration

Wait here a minute,
    I'll bring your gifts—
    ribbons for your branches,
    buckets of water, and
    a wheelbarrow of mulch.

Happy Arbor Day!

Miss Willow

I was spending a delicious spring afternoon
     trailing my slim green leaves
     in the still cool waters,

gazing at my loveliness—
     such elegance!
     such perfection!

—when along came Heron,
     who landed
     in the middle

     of my glorious reflection. . . .

                         Splash.

Tree Traffic

Major tree traffic today—
commuters in both directions,

rippling up and down,
tails unfurled.

The treeway is
heavily squirreled.

Bridge

This tree across the stream
is a trickier bridge
than it might seem.

Quick quickly skipping
or slow slip tiptoe,
it's a wet and mossy,
often soggy
crossing.

No Breakfast

The only leaves left
grow on the highest branches—
the deer walk away.

Beaver Dam

Do you see gnawed trees
        piled up like trash?
Did you see
        a quick brown flash?
Did you hear
        a splash?

Must be that architectural team
with another scheme
to redesign the stream.

Maple Shoot in the Pumpkin Patch

Remember me?
I helicoptered past
your kitchen window last fall,
then hovered over the pumpkin patch.

I had traveled far on the wind that day,
spinning the whole entire way.
I really hadn't planned to stay,

only wanted to look around,
lay my dizziness down,
rest a moment on the ground.

No wind came to carry me aloft,
the dirt was sweet and soft—
I guess
I must
have
dozed
off. . . .

Tree Horse

My tree horse shakes
his rustling green mane,
arches his neck,
plunges his head down,
whinnies sharply.

His taut muscles strain.
I hold on tightly
as he rears up—
we leap into the wind,
vaulting toward sky.

At Night

At night,
when a branch scratches
against the screen,

I lie in bed listening
as my tree whispers:

*Night is happening
outside your window.*

Tree's Place

Tree has staked its claim,
anchoring itself firmly to Earth.
Tree owns this place in the universe.
Within this space, all belongs to Tree—
turf, shaft of air, even slices of sun.
Tree will not step aside for anyone.
Tree stands its ground.
When you
meet Tree,
you *must*
go around.

Fly Fishing in the Crystal River

I hitch up my waders
   step into the cold river
   let out some line
   gather up the slack
   pull my rod back
   snap my wrist
   and catch

          a pine.

Leaving Woods' Lake, Colorado

I have it all planned.
The pines will ride in the back seat
    with the windows down.
The lake and the rowboats
    in the front.
I'll sit in the middle between
    the squirrels and the dinner bell.
I'll lash the log cabin
    with the red gingham curtains
    to the roof.

I'll carry the columbine
    in my lap.
My brothers will ride home
    in the trunk.

Sketchbook on Easel

Slowly,
the wind lifted
pages of the artist's
sketchbook so the birds in the tree
could see.

Between Two Trees

Summer
fills the
empty space
between
two trees
with a
hammock.

Knotholes

I'm glad that
our new fence
came from
a tree
with lots
and lots
of knotholes.
Not for naught
are these
knotholes,
because
if there
were not
lots of knotholes,
I could not
peer through
and spy
on
you.

Poaching

The neighbor's fruit tree
has come to visit, bringing
ripe plums for dessert.

Cooperation

Since there are two horses
and only one tree
in the pasture,

an agreement was made
to *share* this narrow
strip of shade.

So, Molly and Ed,
both rather plump,
stand side by side

muzzle to rump
rump to muzzle—
like a jigsaw puzzle.

Kings Canyon

There is a doorway
     into this ancient Sequoia
     that is just the right size
     for me to step inside—

     I hear its heartbeat.
     I breathe tree.

Lullaby

Tree sighs softly
as the birds patter about
her heavy old branches,
settling down,
tucking their heads
beneath their wings.

She waits until dusk
has shadowed her leaves,
and when she's sure
she's heard that last
soft cheep,

she rocks her birds to sleep.

This Blue Spruce

This blue spruce
arrived today
in a coffee can—
a scrawny sprig
of prickles.

Someday,
it will grow taller
than the house.

Someday,
this blue spruce
will scratch sky.

Autumn

All summer long,
trees studied the sun
to learn the secret
of her fire.

First, they practiced
tracing sunset rays
along their ribs
in colors remembered
from hot summer days.

Now, their chance
on center stage—
they rage yellow gold red,
setting the hills ablaze.

Storm

Last night, wind howled.
Lightning cracked.
Before the thunder's boom,
we heard a crash.
Our tallest tree had snapped
and lay across the lawn—
a schooner's mast
tossed by wild waves
in an ocean of grass.

This morning, all that I can see
is a lot more sky
and a broken tree.

Street Tree

All day long, I stand
here on the street,
neatly clipped
a round-headed shape,

minding my manners.
I know my proper place.
I don't spill leaves,
never dribble sap.

So meek and polite,
no one knows that
when all the cars go home—
when I'm standing here, alone—

I dream wild.
I am *forest*.

Destiny

Some trees will become
     Grandfather Clocks
     Carousel Horses
     Grand Pianos
     Podiums or Front Porches
     Totem Poles
     or Cathedral Doors with
          Intricate Latches.

Others, pencils, toothpicks, or ordinary
          kitchen matches.

Avalanche

A thousand pines are sprawled
like broken toys,
snapped like toothpicks
by the crushing mass of snow
that pounded down
the steep mountain.
They tell me it was over
in minutes, a forest
that took a century to grow
gone in a roar,
an enormous thunder of snow.

Broken String

The winter shows me
how cleverly the trees have
captured wayward kites.

Old Elm Speaks

It is as I told you, Young Sapling.

It will take
autumns of patience
before you snag
your
first
moon.